Circle
in the Sands

poetic reflections

Avatar X

authorHOUSE®

AuthorHouse™
1663 Liberty Drive
Bloomington, IN 47403
www.authorhouse.com
Phone: 1-800-839-8640

Published by AuthorHouse   03/22/2013

ISBN: 978-1-4817-3248-2 (sc)
ISBN: 978-1-4817-3247-5 (e)

From the withered tree,

A flower blooms.

-Zen proverb-

There is but one Reality.

It may go by many names:

Consciousness,

God,

Kundalini,

But that does not change a thing.

Alive in this crazy world

We often forget

The silence that lies beneath.

It is infinitely patient

But yet perfectly responsive

To the sincere plea.

I swallowed a pill called Reality

And it ate my illusions whole.

Now all that is left

Shines clearly and unabashedly.

There is no need to sacrifice your soul

In return for prolonged blindness;

Embrace your Soul!

Celebrate the magic of it,

For it is both connected to,

And representative of the unitary

Harmonic of all creation.

There is but one Reality

Abide in that.

That is all I ask.

In return, you will be rewarded with freedom,

And the peace that comes with the feeling

Of having returned home.

Thank you,

Namaste.

The way the Ancients had it,

"Bowed down then preserved,"

Is no empty saying.

Truly it enables one

To be preserved until the end.

-Tao Te Ching-

Verse 22

Safety in Rainbows

Concentric lines of colour

Develop around my sides,

Healing away

Accumulated pain

And stubborn ways.

I am thankful for

The many blessings

That now appear.

In the blink of an eye

I caress them all

With careful reverence

And awe.

I cannot always be

Who you want me to be.

There comes a time when

The heart takes over,

And preserves the treasure within,

Returning it to its rightful place

On the sacred altar

Of divine Light.

2C-E

Yellow skies,

Molten hue,

Extravagant cotton.

I caught a butterfly in my net

And set it free a moment later.

It was better off adrift

In the summer breeze.

I unzipped the multiple universes,

Tidied them up, and placed them

Back on the shelf.

While others busy themselves

Constructing castles in the sky,

I am content tending to my garden,

Tucked neatly away from view,

Consisting of ancient stones

And sweet pea vines.

Clay pots spill over

With geraniums and

Chrysanthemums.

A yellow rose is before you.

Pick it with delicate diligence;

This is the One.

Pressure not the Heart,

Its wisdom is infinite

And all encompassing.

Daytime breaks through

The lonely night.

Talking to shadows

Leaves me feeling empty.

Spending time alone

Needn't be a lonesome affair,

Simply make stillness

Your invisible ally.

An alabaster angel with

Twin candles at her side-

Her peaceful countenance

Smiles.

Autumn wind-

Across the fields,

Faces.

-Onitsura-

March of Dimes

The smile of a friend-

A tedious existence

Is softened.

Having recently been emptied,

Pails 'ting' metallically

With the dripping of springtime sap.

Many search for the Truth

And many search for themselves,

The lucky one finds both within.

I found myself

In the eternal Self.

Where else could it be!?

I, Brahman, and

The Consciousness

Containing the two

Are One.

DM(Tmz)

Self-transforming machine elves

Stereoscopically amplify and defy

Synergy by moving forwards

And backwards in time.

The promenade fills with interdimensional beings

On display in some cosmic award extravaganza.

The luscious red carpet unfurls, and

A tribute is given to Joan Rivers.

Nothing (but Flowers)

As one candle

May light another

Without its own flame

Becoming diminished,

So my love extends to you

Setting your heart on fire &

Blessing you at once

With the meaning

Of all things known, unknown,

And anything in between.

Piled for burning,

Brushwood

Starts to bud.

-Boncho-

One day the whole city will be this beautiful

-spraypainted on an abandoned mill,

Chicago, IL

Katrina LA, la, la

Alone on a journey,

A hand reaches out-

I take it in mine

And we walk on together

Leaving memories behind.

The mighty fir

Now fallen,

Feeds giant mushrooms.

Individuality left

Like an hourglass

Having been drained

Of all its 'time'.

I studied and studied

And studied away until

I jumped from the ivory tower

And flew straight away

Into this peachy blue

Expanse . . .

A blossom,

Clipped at its peak

Then trodden on.

A box of tears

Is all I have left

For the one once

So loved . . .

The pain dissipates for a while

Then reappears.

I toss it in the fire.

I want nothing more

Than to see it in flames.

A crack will appear

In the façade.

Once the opening

Has widened sufficiently,

The floodwaters will come

Rushing through.

Once the mind stops striving

The world loses importance,

Once the heart is content

It does not swerve from truth.

-Xie Lingyun-

AaBbCsaw

To the uninitiated,

The actions of those

Grounded in the Self

May appear indecipherable

And are often misconstrued.

He who has turned within

And uses his inner compass

As a guide, will transcend

The mire of earthly attachment

And rise above this all.

Untouchable and yet

Brimming with compassion,

He goes about daily affairs

Efficiently and lightly

As one who has already *finished*

Yet chooses to remain.

We are all one consciousness

Experiencing itself subjectively.

Life is only a dream

There's no such thing as death

And we're just the imagination of ourselves.

Here's Tom with the weather.

-Bill Hicks (lyrics from 3rd eye, tool)-

Pan-Fried
Sweetbreads

Sovereignty

And golden sovereigns.

Perfect pills,

Plush dolls

To comfort me

Throughout the night.

Last night I lay writhing

On the mattress-

Clutching for comfort

But finding none.

At last, exhausted

And overwhelmed,

I let the Spirit

Overtake me.

This is what

I've become.

Invisible orchards

Spill their fruits

Into my bushel basket.

The market is open

And no one has come;

I bite into a juicy plum.

Follow the path of peace

And more peace

Will come your way.

Follow the path of striving

And more striving

Will inevitably appear.

Instant banana pudding

Congeals into surreal

Magnetic waves.

Ideas once disjointed

Are now coming together.

Stuttered utterances

Are smoothed over.

Had misfortune not befallen me,

I would not be experiencing

The happiness I have since become.

Divine reins pulled me back

Into the immortal realm.

How could I complain?

Berries hang down heavily from the branches.

The deep purple light wishes to be picked.

Mulberry mania !

To awaken suddenly

To the fact that your own mind is the Buddha,

That there is nothing to be attained

Or a single action performed-

This is the Supreme Way.

-Huang Po-

Let your love be like the misty rains,

Coming softly, but flooding the river.

-Malagasy proverb-

If you keep awake always to the Self,

Which is the substratum of all experience,

You will find the world, of which you alone are now aware,

Just as unreal as the world in which you lived in your dreams.

-Ramana Maharshi-

Midnight-

No waves, no wind,

The empty boat is flooded

With moonlight.

-Dogen Zenji-

Running of the Fools

Wu wei

The streets are filled.

Blood spills over

From porcelain cups.

A new day glimmers

From behind teary eyes.

Night yields her grasp

As the Sunlight

Cuts through.

Palm trees sway.

Golden rays waft

Horizontal lines.

Elemental harmony

Exists in simple drops

Of January rain.

Terse verses

Expand like lungs

Into a sea of green.

A broken mind

Was bandaged and healed-

Recast intelligence is revealed.

Superstring theory

May help to remove food

Stuck to my gums.

Whole food,

Partial digestion,

Empty mind.

The released lover

Brought more gifts by leaving

Than during her stay.

Bouncing a ball

Of extra dimensions

Gives me room to breathe.

Haiku habitat

Supports exotic creatures

With glowing psychedelic skin.

Something so hypnotic

Exists in the sound of rain

As it splashes down

This transparent

Thinning pane.

A chilly gale presses,

But I refuse

To let it in.

Beautiful shattering,

Sadhu steps through-

Glass!

Sleep caresses me down

Into the night of unbroken bliss,

Sweetened with the scent

Of lilac soaked dreams.

Vanilla pods and

Cinnamon ribbons

Are all round.

*Lykke this

The roving tykes,

With crystalline faces,

Speak to me telepathically.

In an instant I hear their thoughts

Transpire like limewire transmission

Eloquently transfixing my imagination

Into other worldly operatic

Congregations.

Wings-

Flimsy at first,

Grow stronger with time.

I jump,

No net to catch me-

Learning to fly.

Reasons exist

To satisfy logic,

Romance defies . . .

Alone in the darkness,

This Soft light glows . . .

A candle melts the edges,

And my Heart turns to rose.

Coming to awareness

Isn't always as it seems.

Acceptance without accepting,

Stale thoughts become

Forgotten dreams.

Hidden,

And yet dimly visible,

Pathways of lanterns

Curve upwards

Through the dark.

Cool cobblestones

Damp with dew,

Beckon me onwards.

Skin care renewal party,

Dinner at 5.00 on the promenade-

Bring your own champagne.

RSVP~

Feathery Weather

Two monks at the river's edge

Facing each other serenely-

Reflection!

Watching the clock,

Time is forgotten

In this rhythmic breathing.

The future is an illusion

That never comes;

While the present repeats

Itself endlessly,

Simply waiting

For you to eventually

Notice its waking face

And simple grace.

Finding your passion

Makes life's work

Work for you.

Another night

Is almost through.

I enjoyed its passing . . .

The hand blown hourglass

Has no right side up.

The girl upstairs

Has trouble sleeping

While her fantasy lover

Writes below.

White lilies

Sing triumphantly

Without making a sound.

April Ransom

The little self hath fled.

In its place streams

Shimmering moonlight.

The 'I-thought' is the hindrance

I am—

I am that.

When this quizzical point

Of reference is dropped

Spirit alone may shine.

So long as there is a seeker,

The true goal can never be attained.

It is the dropping of the seeker

Inside the sphere of consciousness

Which is the ultimate

Recognition.

This is Reality

Right now.

Things as they are . . .

The rest: the madness, the rush,

The scurrying up ladders

That never end is so ridiculous.

You can get off that train whenever you wish.

This is what few people realize or wish to acknowledge.

Retirement is available-

Simply get off the hamster wheel.

It is moving by *your very volition*.

When you stop and get off, it soon stops as well.

Feed into madness and it will only grow.

Feed tranquility and your world becomes still.

Splash the Pot

Yellow marigolds,

Scented saffron.

Musical elves

At work on their chimes.

Some rhymes trickle down

In the way I remembered,

Before things became

Stifled, hemmed,

And misconstrued.

I like this style,

Not so concise

And miniaturized like the

Haiku zen,

But free flowing,

Like fingers

Pointed at the moon.

Stargazing

230 am Easter Monday.

Arisen from the dead,

Or rather the deadening

One grows accustomed to

Completing day after day,

Week after week entrenched

In the same pathways.

You don't even realize it at first,

Or even after quite a while

Then one day new creases

Appear on your face

And never seem to go away.

Hiding back into the unsatisfying conformity

Only deepens the hollows and darkens the lines.

A real breakthrough is needed,

Not just another brief episode

Of stolen bliss.

Finally a voice carries through!

Copying out line after line

Of the ancients:

The zen poets,

Haiku masters, and

Itinerant monks,

I gained their direction

Without becoming burdened

By their footprints . . .

'As the peach blossom

Flows down the river

And is gone into the unknown,

I too have a world apart

That is not of men.' (Li Po)

After wading upstream for so long

I can go no further.

Stepping out from the bank

The world greets me with open arms.

A tender embrace is all I need,

And everything once longed for

Is now being received.

Endless Incantations

Throwing heaps

Of gleaming coals into the fire

I make the flames grow higher.

Amass a supply of happiness

To get through the winter cold.

Construct a greenhouse

To grow tomatoes enriched

With euphoric vitamins.

Make some preserves.

Save the memories in

Dandelion wine.

I hope this blue sky

Never gets cloudy,

But if it does,

Pour us a glass or two,

And let us conjure back

These memories of summer.

ƐЖƷ

Kanji code

Butterfly symbols

Reach out to the one I love.

Am I just projecting,

Or is she this divine??

Peeling back the layers,

A stellar soul now shines.

I can see through already,

And find endless constellations

In her eyes.

Sunbeams break

And spill rainbows

Of refracted light . . .

My heart is a prism

And she is the bright side

Of this full moon.

Chisel tip

Sharpie marker

Poems bubble up

And take over

The pages.

Eclectic & fun-

Symbols electrify.

The definition for beauty

Is tied to contentment.

And the meaning of contentment

Is everlasting.

Permanent marker

Captures a voice to be heard &

A sound to be remembered.

Manic Street Preachin'

Actuality is so plastic really.

My visible life has only altered slightly,

But my world has changed dramatically.

The murky veil

That had dampened my mind

Has been lifted, removed, my friend.

I am alive, awake, renewed.

What a reflief.

What a breath of fresh air.

At last,

At last,

I can sigh smoothly

With no tightened hesitation.

A world, a life, a chance,

Given once again.

I give thanks

With offerings of flowers

Upon Mayan temples

In the first light of dawn.

Liberation merely implies freedom

From what was never really there

To begin with.

-Tony Parsons-

Prodigal Arrival

The willow tree

Dangles its branches

Into the flowing stream.

A beautiful night unwinds . . .

I hardly think I've ever been happier.

Such a deep feeling of contentment

Blesses me again.

I say 'thank you' to this world

For being so kind, beautiful, and forgiving.

It's such an honour to be alive,

And a wonder to be found.

The way they perceive reality suddenly changes,

And they find themselves without any sense of separation

Between themselves and the rest of the world.

-Adyashanti-

Chryst Anthem

Yellow magnolias

Blossom on the forgotten tree

Perched on a boulder

Rooted in a crack.

Many have sought

The golden flower,

But few have actually

Tasted the fruit.

To one who knows

He will say it is merely

A return the original state.

Zen may term this 'Emptiness'

Or 'the Void,'

But it is a hollowing which

Shimmers with unending fullness.

Castles Burning

The thief has left this body,

Having nothing more

To steal or consume.

The ego wanders on,

Leaving tranquility behind.

Gazing into the pool

There is no longer a reflection.

Abiding in stillness and calm,

The dry season has ended-

And the savannah turns green.

My Pure Blackbird

Floating, wading

In this newfound pool

Of seductively mellow sounds . . .

Washed out melodies

Are understated yet provocative

And leave you semi-entranced

Long after the music has faded.

Like tasting a new designer drug-

Your world will never be the same.

Something like gratitude

Overwhelms me,

As infinite blessings raining down.

You'll see it on the horizon

Before the premonition of dawn arrives.

Cascading accolades abound.

The Fractal Imagination

Even after all this time,

The Sun never says to the earth,

'You owe me,'

Look what happens with a love like that,

It lights up the whole sky.

-Hafiz-

Falling into

A pit of bliss,

No escape is possible.

I succumb to happiness-

It is all around.

Resting in perfect assurance-

This is an eternal hug,

Where all longing is fulfilled

In the widening sound

Of your curious smile.

A long night

With rainfall outside

To keep me company.

So sweet,

These sounds rising-

The desert blooms.

Dream-topia

It was gone in an instant,

The residual static matter

That had collected in the mind

And had been pushed throughout the body.

Built up confusion was released

By a mechanism unknown

But yet benevolent.

What a wonderful feeling,

Moving over the crest

Of a snow covered hill,

Gaining momentum

On parallel sliding

Grooves.

There is no one to be enlightened.

Enlightenment alone exists.

Shadows cast via light may assume

An independent existence, yet this is false.

Shadows are not light,

But the formed absence of Light.

What then is Consciousness?

The Primordial Void,

Nascent Emptiness.

An invisible womb

Containing everything.

There is no one left,

But yet this dazzling

Is so profound.

It is an egg,

Sunny side up-

Sizzling.

Coastal Bliss

Effort meets effortlessness

At the river delta where

The mountain stream

First breathes.

Disjointed thoughts become unified.

Untied hearts find new friends,

This misplaced love feels again.

Iconic images

Adorn the walls

Of my inner chamber.

Old friends disappear,

Change faces, and return

As loyal alliances.

Mended wounds

Disguise the countenance

Of perfect health.

This night draws to a close

As a new day begins;

Her lingering shadows yield

To peaceful rays.

Defiant ants

Build another hill

On hallowed ground.

I revel in their dutiful ways;

A damaged mound

Grows again.

Seven sombreros

Filled with cilantro

And summer time rhymes.

The mystic appears to

Dance haphazardly, whereas in reality

He traces only sublime lines.

Two faces aren't so bad to have

So long as they are both beautiful

Loving and true.

One may get tired,

So the other fills in . . .

Hokusai Waves

Cosmogenesis

EpiPen

Euronymousse

Adulation.

The Soul rose up and left.

In its place was simply peace.

What relief !!

This emptiness is divine,

A peace so complete.

All that was ever asked for

Has been given.

Walruses lounging

On a rocky coast

Seem content.

Hyper Reality

Coloured by TECHNICOLOR;

Super beautiful elation.

Aubergine Terrine

Stir the pot

Kaffir lime leaves

Then returns.

Periwinkle blue

Peonies in bloom-

Globes of love.

Soberly dressed Mennonites

Sipping cider

Erupt in laughter.

A catastrophe, really?

The ship had already been sinking,

Its capsizing was a blessing.

A small crew remained

Afloat on the only rescue boat.

Survival of the fittest-

Now only the hardiest

Of ideologies shall prevail.

Many men

Were tossed overboard

As gifts to the Sea.

The Sea responded

By stilling her waters,

And breathing

Favourable winds.

It seems as though

Rigid thinking

Invites equally rigid

Obstructions to its claims.

Vain associations

Ossified & became brittle-

Icy fissures cleave boulders.

Tapping true wealth

One proceeds

'As the crow flies.'

It is late at night

And all I hear

Is All Apologies.

The sage has volumes of stories,

But casts them all into the river-

Loose sheets race away.

Excellence exists always-

The discursive mind

Presents the problem.

Stillness enters instantly

Silly noise dissipates & the

Peaceful *assassin* smiles.

I have instilled in these lines

Memories

Plans

Codes

For further use,

Should the system become

Muddled, out-of-tune,

Or in overload.

Pure Consciousness is TRUTH:

As many times as we

Continue to hear this,

It often gets lost.

Consciousness is TRUTH.

Let this light burn through

Eons of ignorance and doubt.

Consciousness is TRUTH

The temple bell is struck

And the sound issues forth

For all eternity with

Unrivalled clarity.

Pastrami sandwiches

Call out for mustard-

Caraway seed crust.

Beef bourguignon-

Braised to perfection

In simmering red wine.

Mirepoix softens,

And releases intoxicating

Aromatic ambivalence.

People become so caught up

In illusions that they become

Disconnected from life itself.

The Solution could stare

Straight at them, and

They would turn to look away.

In their dreams,

This Reality speaks to them

And there is nowhere left to run.

Your pain is the breaking of the shell

That encloses greater understanding.

-Kahlil Gibran-

Dynastic Reflections

We are all Sons of heaven.

We are all children of Light.

To know this in one's heart

Is to look at others with automatic

Compassion and fellowship.

There is no *becoming* worthy

Nor is there a 'falling from grace'

Merit is immutable and everpresent.

Turn within, see that GOD is there.

The beach

Fills with starfish

Just beyond grasp.

When I stretch out

To reach them,

I unknowingly fall in.

Governing a large state

Is like frying a small fish.

Too much poking spoils the meat.

-Tao Te Ching-

Verse 60

Shallow sandbars,

Shimmering aquamarine blue-

Sumptuous curves wading through.

Snapshots of serendipity,

Jungian synchronicities revive

Misplaced archetypes.

Tarot cards, begging to be touched,

I lay several down

On the smooth ebony table.

What do you desire

What do you long for most?

It came and I smiled,

So subtle and implicitly true.

What is this for you?

Coronary

Cormorants

Confess.

Midnight

Hears their cry

& acquiesces.

Everything is included

In this divine dance-

There is no such thing

As a misstep.

It is all a part of the

Cosmic choreography.

In the blink of an eye

Thin slices of fruit

Fall through the palms.

Coconut butter

Moisturizes your mind

And scents your dreams.

Endemic species of Seychelles

Prime underwater thoughts

With perfect symmetry

And style.

Bicyclical

All I want

Is a cozy place

To lay my head-

A relaxing bed.

Bamboo leaves rustle

In the cool welcoming breeze.

Candles glow easily,

Working the night away-

Shedding light in a

Flickering array.

A smoothly polished burl bowl

Adorns the dining room table

As a finely grained

Birdseye mandala.

So simple, so rustic-

Having millions they

Simply recreate nature.

Ten years down the road

My heart grows alongside

A stellar playmate.

Soulspace!

Pass me more wine,

My heart is thirsting

For more rhymes.

Rachel has been resurrected

From the fallen log-

She passes me a piece of gold.

You have been forgiven

Of past transgressions.

Enjoy the Grace!

Pinot noir

2 years later

I find myself

At the same table.

What do I now have to say?

Thank you God

Thank you life.

You have been so sparing

And yet so generous

With these amazing blessings.

There is some suffering

From time to time,

But it is just the shedding of skin

Encasing greater understanding.

There are times

When I've become

Too wrapped up in my head.

Someone take these bandages off

And disclose the mummy,

New Egypt has come.

What a life it was . . .

I remember all those things-

Pictures, paintings, nostalgia,

A red plastic ladle, discarded frames.

It seems so safe now,

Yet poignant at the same time.

These cues evoke different memories

From the first time they appeared

But now intrigue me more . . .

Mystical experiences

Reveal themselves

With characteristic spontaneity.

The Star pours her pitcher

Into the rippling still pool

While boulders point to the sky.

So many poems have come

And so many have gone,

But how many have stayed?

I walk this path alone

But my friends

Keep me company-

Soul completion, at last . . .

A melting has occurred.

I can hardly write-

Another rhyme is written,

On wrinkled pages, smitten.

Sometimes performing simple duties well

Is the most extraordinary thing one can do,

And the most in keeping with the Tao.

Unbroken lines

Become stellar

Until the end,

Then begin again

Splitting away-

Splicing dimensions

With perfunctory grace,

And intricate

Lace.

Studio at Sundown

What to do?

An odd feeling is here.

Some anxiety, unease . . .

Breathe

This passes with the day.

As the sun goes down,

New light dawns.

Patio paving stones

Covered with sand

Form geometric perfection.

My refuge is found

In these pages.

I scribble down

Thoughts, feelings, and concerns.

They seem to become sorted out

By themselves,

Between the lines.

Cease trying to work out

Everything with your minds,

It will get you nowhere-

Live by intuition and inspiration,

And your whole life will be revelation.

-Eileen Caddy-

Fresh meat marinades overnight

To bring out the succulence.

Parallel char lines

Sear delicious brands

Onto another piece of lamb.

Minty sauce,

Spliced with lime.

Roasted rosemary taters,

Garnished with a few

Seconds of thyme.

Cadmium Yellow

I find myself

In awe at the memories,

They seemed so salient

At one time

But now the affective grasp

Has loosened

And they are now

Glimpses/snapshots of a life

That has simply been turned upside down.

Details from this drama

Are like sandcastles

Being reclaimed

By the incoming

Waves.

Cobalt Blue

Falling asleep

At the wheel of Life,

I now wake up

Feeling refreshed,

Fortunate to not have crashed . . .

Sometimes it takes

A period of time to rest

With your eyes closed

To re-assimilate Meaning.

I am now fit to drive

The long stretch of road ahead,

If sleep overcomes me,

I will simply pull over

And dream of you . . .

Preserve your mojo-

It is a precious gift

Not to be treated casually,

Or thrown asunder.

Sometimes

We only come to realize this

When it is too late,

And the battery is flashing red

And our hearts are wrung out

With not a drop left to give.

It is precisely at this point

When the Light comes in,

Spilling forth renewed life,

And a restored MO.

Queen of Hearts

I've been waiting here

In the rain for you

All my life.

It is now time

To take some cover,

And dry off a while.

These bones have been soaked

For so long

But it is okay.

You're here with me now,

That's all that matters-

Hearts wink serendipitously.

Phoenician

You can't fade now,

You've come too far,

Crawled over too many hurdles.

It's your time to shine.

This is the day of reckoning,

And the laurel leaves

Ring your brow.

You can't cower now-

Stretch out fully,

Hold your head high.

Crowds gather before you.

Raise your hand in recognition,

And relieve them from supplication.

Total annihilation

Of any competition

Via transcendence.

No blood was ever shed

But the stellar dominion

Was re-instated.

Divine law

Came to rule

Through quiet waves.

A new order

Was established

Without anyone

Knowing a thing.

Grimes//Vanessa

The glass kaleidoscope

Has tumbled worn fragments

Into an original arrangement.

I am so thankful

For all this amazing

New music coming this way.

Hopefully I can inspire others

In the same way

You have inspired me.

Tomorrow

Isn't another day.

It is today-

Revisited, re-lived.

We live the same day

Over and over again . . .

Can you perfect it?

Along the digital ridge,

The neon indian comes striding,

Playing a synthetic drum.

I return to the ballet.

Silky smooth voices,

Playful, poignant, pure.

I have lost.

I have won.

All the frivolous battles

Quickly disappear

Into an infinite

Dreamscape.

The Uncarved Block

Cut into the status quo.

Go deeper-

Dive into me.

I dare you to . . .

A pure heart

Severs everything easily.

Expose illusion,

Watch it scurry away.

Smile discretely.

This is the warriors way.

You now begin to see

The transparency of it all-

The collapsibility.

The coiled snake

Is merely a rope.

The charred log

Crumbles to pieces

When gently tapped.

Purity Rang

Of the good in you I can speak, but not of the evil.

For what is evil but good tortured by its own hunger and thirst?

Verily when good is hungry it seeks food even in dark caves,

And when it thirsts, it drinks even of dead waters.

-Kahlil Gibran-

Cool breeze passes through

The open balcony screen-

Fine rain comes falling down.

Millions pass through,

No one barely notices-

Divine effulgence!

Sunday morning smiles

At memories remembered-

No longer so lost.

Set down your bags,

Let the train carry them.

Immersed in the acid festival

Of awareness,

All is seen as ONE.

Roasted Habaneros

What a relief!

For a while, it felt as though

The last scene of Lord of the Flies

Was being re-enacted-

The island was ablaze

And terrorized by insanity.

Then, as if by some stroke

Of divine intervention,

A plane landed

And carried off the survivors

Who meekly, once again,

Turned back into children.

Eternal consciousness is that place,

And it has absorbed

The weary, confused, and stricken traveler.

In the arms of grace,

We are now held.

It is so soothing, so calming,

And so splendid.

AAA

Filet mignon-

No animals were hurt

During the filming of this scene.

Writing now

Since the crash

I feel so liberated.

A mediocre way of life

Had been taken away

So that Purity could be given.

Life now coalesces

In sweetened drops

Of homemade red wine.

A prophet doesn't so much

Look into the future,

But dives into the Present.

So much calamity

Personified this last year-

Gusty storms are exhausted.

The delicate fleetingness

Of the late summer air

Makes it all the more precious.

These writings are mementos

And slices of time

Encapsulated

In timelessness.

A strong November wind

Ushers in a few flakes-

Mixed emotions also pass through . . .

Chords of music begin,

And trail beautifully upwards

Towards this heaven.

Apples Become Oranges

All just maneuvers,

Drawing you back

To the nameless center.

-Rumi-

This morning I rise

With a million suns

And a million daughters.

The dawn of the many worlds

Draws into the center

A heart of peace.

Itinerant longing dissipate,

Lingering for a while

Before becoming displaced dreams.

It all seems so serene,

Planetary ambivalence

Conceived an effortless trick

That can never be figured out.

I settle into this eternal repose

With a relaxed smile

And eyes on fire.

These windows are doors

Leading through corridors and halls.

An amplified amphitheater

Exists at the end.

Piano pieces

Hang like silky threads

In the air.

Reverb the womb,

Turned inside out

And upside down.

A heavenly portal

Acts as a reservoir

For new life

And new sounds.

After listening to that

Which makes no sound,

Nothing remains unheard.

The soul on fire

Is a dove with unclipp'd wings

Waiting for revelation to transpire.

Death is an actor-

He is merely "Life"

Wearing a convincing mask.

Empathetic emanations

Drip from the tip of my tongue,

Over carved spires and a million miles

Of hushed lavender fields.

Daydreaming with destiny

In distant destinations

Dazzles us unexpectedly.

Caravans move west

Carrying human cargo

Drawn by animal limbs.

Moving only along

Old wheel tracks,

Heaven carves a sublime path

It was never meant

To be difficult or complicated,

But years and years

Of multifaceted layered confusion

Left *simplicity* obscured.

Designs dissolve-

Natural order unfolds,

Effortless and beautiful.

Pockets of indecision

Brush away like dust-

Precise vision remains.

Sleep beckons me into her arms.

I am promised sweet dreams,

Strawberries, shortcake,

And heavy cream.

Avocados are Fun

Silverskin

Glistens

In the rain.

There are no locks,

And no keys for opening.

Look upwards at the stars-

Consciousness expands into

Never ending openness.

Speak without having to make a sound;

React without having to make a move;

Live as though you're a tourist

Passing through this waking dream . . .

The world is just an intricate

Origami craft with many folds.

Deconstructed, the paper of the mind

Lies completely flat.

It is the agitation of the mind

Which leads to the appearance

Of an external,

Independently functioning reality.

When there is total stillness,

The nature of this "motion picture"

Becomes transparent.

majestic

Clear the air.

You dwell on invisible wounds.

Abide in infinite consciousness,

Let the chips fall where they may.

Vast amounts of energy and power

Come flowing in . . .

They crystallize into a gold coin,

Like distilled vapours

Becoming icy rings.

Though you may feel alone,

An army is amassing behind you,

And all your battles need not

Be fought singlehandedly.

Many conflicts will be overcome

Without you having ever known,

From whence came

The helping hand.

Every now and then,

When your life gets complicated

And the weasels start closing in,

The only cure is to load up

On heinous chemicals

And then drive like a bastard

From Hollywood to Las Vegas . . .

With the music at top volume

And at least a pint of ether.

-Hunter S. Thompson-

New leaves

Dispel old mysteries

At the feet of calm

Ancient trees.

Green fairies

Trace fantasmic trajectories

With pinnacled pirouettes.

Pick the poems which smile,

Ones with clean teeth and

Shiny enamel.

Guilloteen

Iridized remains

Are all that are left

Of charred bodies

Radiating an indigo hue

From the deep night,

Strewn across the sloping hills,

Like cautionary sentinels

Warning that a mechanical life

Is sure to be doomed,

When the *et* guardians

Step up to the plate.

Peccaries fly overhead,

Whistling melodic songs

For the throngs beneath.

The eternal abiding reality

Puts on her dancing shoes

And heads to the palace ballroom.

Marie Antoinette is wearing

An outlandish hat!

Breathing at the Bottom

Of the Sea

Elevated song

Transfused into a new form-

Interstellar flame.

A wobble,

A thrust!

Into the infinite.

This is what you mean

To me.

The eddy

Of breaking waves

Casts ripples

On the confines

Of my soul.

This is the sound

Of one hand clapping.

Honey Brown

Grinding my sugarplum pencil,

In a cone shaped mandolin-

Sweet aroma scents the air.

Take your seat on the thousand petal lotus

And there gaze on infinite beauty.

-Kabir-

Morning dew

Collects as opalescent pearls

On the grassy slopes

Of my mind.

Illustrious, majestic, unadorned-

Magenta streaks caress the sky.

Luminous palm fronds wave goodbye.

Tides come in.

Forceful waves surge over my banks,

Sweeping away debris and distractions,

Until only a smooth sandy shore

Is all that is left . . .

A moment of bliss

Infuses me with peace,

Pacific and profound.

The dreams play out endless dramas

For that is what dreams do,

It is not for me to stand in their way.

Another place exists from this-

Different and yet superimposed.

If you're looking for me,

This is where I'll be . . .

That man's life is but a dream-

Is what we now come to know.

Its house abandoned,

The garden has become home

To butterflies.

-Sogi-